Nita Mehta's
Taste of GUJARAT

Nita Mehta

B.Sc. (Home Science), M.Sc. (Food & Nutrition) Gold Medalist

Coauthor
Hema B. Watchmaker

SNAB
PUBLISHERS PVT LTD

Nita Mehta's
Taste of GUJARAT

© Copyright 2001-2009 **SNAB** Excellence in Books Publishers Pvt Ltd

7th Print 2009
ISBN 978-81-86004-95-1

Food Styling and Photography: **SNAB** Excellence in Books

Layout and Laser Typesetting :

N.I.T.A. ☎ 23252948
National Information Technology Academy
3A/3, Asaf Ali Road
New Delhi-110002

Published by :

SNAB Excellence in Books
Publishers Pvt. Ltd.
3A/3 Asaf Ali Road,
New Delhi - 110002
Tel: 23252948, 23250091
Telefax:91-11-23250091

Contributing Writers :
Anurag Mehta
Subhash Mehta

Editorial & Proofreading :
Rakesh
Ramesh

Editorial and Marketing office:
E-159, Greater Kailash-II, N.Delhi-48
Fax: 91-11-29225218, 29229558
Tel: 91-11-29214011, 29218574
E-Mail: nitamehta@email.com
nitamehta@nitamehta.com
Website: http://www.nitamehta.com
Website: http://www.snabindia.com

Distributed by :

 NITA MEHTA BOOKS Distributors & Publishers
Head office: 3A/3, Asaf Ali Road, New Delhi - 02
Tel.: 011-23252948, 23250091
Distribution Centre: 011-26813199, 26813200
E-mail: nitamehta@nitamehta.com, gagan@nitamehta.com

Printed by :
PRESSTECH LITHO PVT. LTD.

Rs. 89/-

Introduction

$\mathcal{G}$ujarati cuisine is a vegetarian gourmet's dream come true. It is a true vegetarian wonder with complete nutrition derived from vegetables prepared in innumerable variations and subtly flavoured with spices. The food like the Gujaratis themselves is simple, practical and down to earth. Gujarati cuisine is primarily vegetarian, the main reason being the influence of Jainism.

For the taste of traditional Gujarati cuisine, one has to try the typical Gujarati thali that consists of one variety each of dal and kadhi, two to three vegetables and salad, savories, sweets, puris or phulka rotis, rice, chutneys, pickles and papads. Lunch in a Gujarati home is a feast everyday. Food is mildly flavoured and is pepped up with plenty of hot pickles and chutneys. The savouries or snacks like khaman dhokla or khandavi which are served with the thali are called "Farsan". Sweets are an inevitable part of a Gujarati menu. A Gujarati lunch is generally served with a glass of Chhaas (butter milk). The Gujaratis generally prefer a light dinner, which consists of theplas and pickles or kadhi and khichdi or handvo or bhakri and one vegetable with gravy.

The cuisine in South Gujarat is spicy where green chillies add life to the food. They use more sugar in their cooking and as a result the cuisine has a sweet tangy flavour.

In Gujarat during winter when green vegetables are available in plenty a delicious vegetable medley called 'Undhiya' is made using potatoes, brinjal, green beans and fenugreek leaf dumplings. This book contains favourite Gujarati recipes all of which have been tried and tested to perfection. Enjoy the 'Taste of Gujarat'!

Nita Mehta

Uniqueness of Gujarati Khaana

- The food is low in calories as very little oil is used in preparing the dishes. The snacks are also generally steamed instead of being fried in oil.

- The food is very quick to prepare and yet tasty. The dishes are very simple to cook.

- Generally onion and garlic are not used. However green chilli -ginger paste is used a lot to flavour the food. To make green chilli-ginger paste, grind together 8 green chillies with 2" ginger piece. This can be stored in the refrigerator for a few days. To make a small quantity of the paste, grind 2 green chillies with ½" ginger.

Names of Ingredients

HINDI	ENGLISH	GUJARATI
Bhindi	Ladies finger	Bhinda
Baingan	Brinjal	Vaingan
Lauki	White gourd	Doodhi
Aloo	Potato	Bataka
Piyaz	Onion	Kanda
Lahsoon	Garlic	Lason
Adrak	Ginger	Aadu
Hari Mirch	Green Chilli	Lilu marchu
Haldi	Turmeric	Haladar
Hara Dhania	Coriander leaves	Kothmir
Matar	Peas	Vatana

Sukha Dhania	Coriander seeds	Suka Dhana
Ajwain	Aniseed	Ajmo
Til	Sesame seeds	Tal
Rai	Mustard seeds	Rai
Jeera	Cumin seeds	Jeera
Laung	Cloves	Lavange
Dalchini	Cinnamon	Taj
Hing	Asafoetida	Hing
Seviyan	Vermicelli	Sev
Moongfali	Ground nut	Sing dana
Gehu ka Atta	Wheat flour	Loat
Besan	Gram flour	Chana no loat
Suji	Semolina	Ravo
Saunf	Fennel	Variali
KhasKhas	Poppy seeds	KhasKhas

Contents

Snacks   **13**

SNACKS

Gujaratis prepare a variety of snacks and some of them are included in meals. They call it Farsan (like patra, Khandvi, Khaman).
Farsan is a must in a Gujarati Thali.

Stuffed Khandvi

Picture on cover   *Serves 6-8*

Easy to make, small stuffed rolls made out gram flour cooked in butter milk.

½ cup besan (gram flour)
½ cup curd (not too sour) mixed with 1 cup water to get 1½ cups butter milk
¼ tsp haldi (turmeric powder), ¼ tsp jeera powder (cumin seeds)
½ tsp dhania powder, a pinch of hing (asafoetida) powder, 1 tsp salt

PASTE
½" piece ginger, 1-2 green chillies

FILLING
1 tbsp oil, ½ tsp rai, 1 tsp kishmish - chopped, 1 tbsp chopped coriander
1 tbsp grated carrot, 2 tbsp grated fresh coconut, 2 pinches salt

CHOWNK (TEMPERING)
1½ tbsp oil
½ tsp rai (mustard seeds), 2-3 green chillies - cut into thin long pieces
a few coriander leaves, 1 tbsp grated fresh coconut

1. Mix besan with 1½ cups buttermilk till smooth. Add haldi, jeera powder, dhania powder, hing, salt and ginger-green chilli paste.
2. Spread a cling film (plastic sheet) on the backside of a big tray.
3. Keep the mixture on low heat in a non stick pan. Cook this mixture for about 25 min, stirring, till the mixture becomes very thick and translucent. Drop 1 tsp mixture on the tray and spread. Let it cool for a while and check if it comes out easily. If it does, remove from fire, otherwise cook for another 5 minutes. Remove from fire.
4. While the mixture is still hot, quickly spread some mixture as thinly and evenly as possible on the cling film. Level it with a knife.
5. For the filling, heat oil. Add rai. After it crackles, add coconut, carrot, kishmish and chopped coriander. Add salt. Mix. Remove from fire.
6. After the besan mixture cools, cut breadthwise into 2" wide strips. Neaten the 4 border lines with a knife. Put 1 tsp filling at one end. Roll each strip, loosening with a knife initially, to get small cylinders.
7. Prepare the tempering by heating oil in a small vessel. Add rai. When rai splutters, add green chillies. Remove from fire and pour the oil on the khandavis arranged in the plate. Garnish with coconut & coriander.

Khata Dhokla

Picture on cover   *Serves 12*

*The delicious, white dhokla made from fermented rice and dal batter.
Vegetables added to it enhance the taste and nutrition.*

BATTER

1½ cups sela or ushna (parboiled) rice
½ cup urad dal (split black beans)
¼ cup sour curds, 2 tsp salt

OTHER INGREDIENTS

1 tsp green chilli-ginger paste, a pinch hing (asafoetida)
½ tsp saboot kali mirch (black peppercorns) - coarsely ground or red chilli pd.
1 tsp sugar, ¼ tsp soda bi-carb, 3/4 tsp eno fruit salt
1½ tbsp oil mixed with 3 tbsp water

VEGETABLES (OPTIONAL)

¼ cup shelled tender peas
¼ cup finely chopped beans and carrots mixed together

1. Soak the rice and urad dal separately overnight or for 7-8 hours, in plenty of water. Drain out water and grind rice with 1 cup water. Drain dal and grind dal very finely with ½ cup water, adding small amounts of water gradually till the dal turns very smooth. After it is ground nicely, grind further till it turns whitish and absolutely smooth.
2. Mix both the batters. Add the sour curds and salt.
3. Allow to ferment in a warm place for 7-8 hours. Ferment till it swells and smells sour. If it does not ferment properly, keep it away for some more time. Do not proceed further.
4. After it is fermented, add asafoetida, green chilli-ginger paste, sugar and vegetables and mix well.
5. Put soda & eno fruit salt in the centre. Heat 3 tbsp water with 1½ tbsp oil and pour over the soda. Wait till bubbles appear. Mix very well.
6. Apply a little oil to a metal thali. Pour half the batter so as to fill half the height of a 7-8" thali. Sprinkle a little ground pepper or red chilli powder on top. Sprinkle some vegetables on top. Steam for about 10-12 minutes. Remove from fire. Cool and cut into pieces. Repeat with the rest of the batter. Serve with coconut or green chutney.

Instant Khaman Dhokla

Picture on page 19   *Serves 6*

Yellow dhokla prepared instantly from besan, eno fruit salt and soda bi-carb.

1½ cups besan (gram flour), 1 cup water
1 tsp sugar, ½ tsp haldi (turmeric powder)
2 tsp chilli-ginger paste
1 tsp salt
¼ tsp soda-bi-carb, 1½ tsp eno fruit salt, 2 tsp lemon juice
1 tbsp oil mixed with 4 tbsp water

TEMPERING
2 tbsp oil, 1 tsp rai (mustard seeds)
2-3 green chillies - slit into 2 long pieces
3/4 cup water, 1 tbsp sugar, 4 tbsp white vinegar
2-3 tbsp freshly grated coconut, 2-3 tbsp chopped coriander

1. Sift besan through fine sieve to make it light and free of any lumps.
2. Mix besan, turmeric powder, salt, sugar, chilli-ginger paste and water to a smooth batter.
3. Grease a 7" diameter thali (a small thali) with oil.
4. Heat 1 tbsp oil with 4 tbsp water and add to the batter. Beat well.
5. Add eno fruit salt and soda-bi-carb to the above batter and pour lemon juice over it. Beat well for a few seconds.
6. Immediately pour this mixture in the greased thali. Level the batter with a knife. Steam for 12-13 minutes on medium heat, when the back of a spoon inserted in the dhokla comes out clean. Remove from fire and leave the dhokla aside for 5 minutes. Do not over steam. It turns dry.
7. Cool and cut into 1½" diamond shaped pieces. Carefully remove the pieces and arrange on the serving platter.
8. To temper, heat oil, add rai. As rai splutters, add green chillies. Add water, sugar and vinegar. Boil for 2 min. Pour tempering on the dhoklas.
9. Sprinkle chopped coriander and freshly grated coconut. Serve after a while so that the water gets absorbed and the dhokla turns soft.

Dakor na Gota

Serves 8

Crisp pakoras, a speciality of the village Dakor, in Gujarat.

2 cups besan (coarse)
2 tbsp chopped methi leaves (fenugreek greens) or coriander
1 tsp red chilli powder, 1 tsp sugar, salt to taste
2 tsp saboot dhania (coriander seeds), 1 tsp saunf
1 tsp saboot kali mirch (black peppercorns),
½ tsp citric acid or 1 tbsp lemon juice, a pinch of soda bi carb
¼ cup milk mixed with ¼ cup water
2 tsp hot oil

1. Mix besan with methi. Add all the ingredients, except the last two.
2. Add milk and water mixture and make a smooth batter like pakodas.
3. Add hot oil to the batter. Allow the batter to stand for 15-20 minutes.
4. Heat oil for frying. Drop teaspoonfuls of batter in hot oil. Fry them on low medium heat till golden brown. Serve with tamarind chutney.

Bataka Vada

Picture on page 19   *Makes 10*

Crisp balls of tempered mashed potatoes coated with gramflour.

½ kg (6 meduim) potatoes - boiled & mashed
½ tsp garam masala
1 tsp lemon juice, ½ tsp sugar, 1½ tsp salt
2 tbsp coriander leaves chopped

PASTE (2 tsp)
2-3 green chillies, 1" piece ginger, 5-6 flakes garlic (optional)

TEMPERING
1 tbsp oil, ½ tsp rai (mustard seeds), a pinch of hing (asafoetida)
¼ tsp haldi (turmeric powder), ½-3/4 tsp chilli powder

BATTER FOR COATING
1 cup besan, 1 tbsp rice flour
¼ tsp turmeric powder, ½ tsp chilli powder, ½ tsp salt

1. Mix mashed boiled potatoes with ginger-garlic-chilli paste.
2. Add lemon juice, salt, sugar, garam masala and coriander leaves.
3. Heat 1 tbsp oil add rai and hing. After the rai splutters remove from fire. Add turmeric and chilli powder to the hot oil and pour this hot tempering over the potato mixture.
4. Mix well and make lemon sized balls from this mixture.
5. Make a thick batter with besan, rice flour and about ½ cup water. Add all the other dry ingredients.
6. Heat enough oil in a kadhai.
7. Fatten the potato vada a little, dip into batter, and deep fry them in hot oil till golden brown.
8. Serve hot with green chutney or tomato ketchup.

Patra

Serves 4

Steamed rolls made from Colocasia (arbi) leaves with gramflour and spices.

10 medium size arbi (colocasia) leaves
2 cups besan (gram flour)
2 tbsp imli (tamarind) pulp, 2 tbsp gur (jaggery)
½ tsp haldi (turmeric powder), 1 tsp red chilli powder
2 tsp dhania powder, ½ tsp jeera powder, 1 tsp garam masala powder
¼ tsp hing (asafoetida) powder,
2 tsp oil, salt to taste

PASTE
2-3 green chillies, ½" piece ginger, 10-12 garlic flakes

CHOWNK (TEMPERING)
2 tbsp oil
1 tsp rai (mustard seeds), 1 tsp til (sesame seeds)
2-3 tbsp chopped coriander for garnish

1. Wash and pat dry leaves. Remove stems.
2. Soak tamarind in water and squeeze out thick pulp.
3. Mix besan with all the other ingredients as well as the ginger- garlic-chilli paste. Add a little water to make a thick paste that can be spread on the leaves.
4. Take the biggest leaf with its lighter side on the top. Spread 1 tbsp batter evenly on the surface of the leaf.
5. Place the next biggest leaf on top of the first leaf and spread the batter on it. Repeat this with 3 more leaves. After all the leaves have been placed together, fold lengthwise from each side.
6. Roll the leaves tightly, starting from the stem end. Make 2 such rolls, each roll made up of 5 leaves.
7. Cook the rolls by steaming in a double boiler or in a pressure cooker. After first whistle, cook on slow heat for 5 to 7 minutes.
8. Cut the roll into ½" thick slices on cooling.
9. To temper, heat oil in a big kadhai. Add rai and til. As the rai starts spluttering, add the patra slices and stir for few minutes.
10. Remove from fire, garnish with coriander leaves and serve hot.

Khaman Dhokla (from channa dal)

Serves 6

Yellow dhokla made out of channa dal which is soaked, ground & fermented.

1 cup chana dal, 1 tsp urad dal
2 tbsp curd, 1¼ tsp salt
1/8 tsp haldi (turmeric powder)
1 tsp green chilli-ginger paste
1 tbsp oil mixed with 1 tbsp water
1 tsp sugar
1 tsp lemon juice, ½ tsp soda-bi-carb

CHOWNK (TEMPERING)
1½ tbsp oil
¼ tsp hing powder, 3/4 tsp rai (mustard seeds)
2-3 green chillies - slit into 2 pieces
1/3 cup water, 1 tsp sugar, 2 tsp lemon juice
2-3 tbsp freshly grated coconut, 2-3 tbsp chopped coriander

1. Clean, wash channa dal and urad dal and soak for 6 to 7 hours or overnight.
2. Drain and grind soaked dals with about 1/3 cup water to a get a thick soft dropping consistency like the batter for cakes or idlis.
3. Add curd and salt to the batter and mix well. Cover the batter and ferment it for 6 to 7 hours.
4. Add haldi, chilli-ginger paste and sugar.
5. Add soda-bi-carb and 1 tsp lemon juice over it.
6. Heat 1 tbsp water and 1 tbsp oil mixed together. Add to the batter. Mix well and beat well for 2 minutes.
7. Immediately put this batter in a greased thali of 1½" height and steam for about 10-12 minutes.
8. Remove from fire and cool. Cut into 1½" diamond shape pieces.
9. To temper, heat 2 tbsp oil in a kadhai, add rai and hing, as rai splutters add green chillies. Add water, sugar and lemon juice. Let it boil and then pour the oil on the dhokla.
10. Garnish with freshly grated coconut and coriander leaves. Serve with green chutney.

Bhelpuri

Picture on facing page   *Serves 6-8*

Bhel made from puffed rice, sev, puris and served with green mint chutney, red garlic chutney and date tamarind chutney.

8 (cups) 100 gm murmura (puffed rice)
1 cup (50 gm) sev namkeen, 1 cup (50 gm) chana dal fried
½ cup (50 gm) roasted groundnuts
12 puris (chat papadis) - broken into small pieces
2 tbsp oil
¼ tsp haldi (turmeric powder), ¼ tsp red chilli powder
1 tbsp salt, or to taste
1 boiled potato - diced, 1 onion - finely chopped
2 tbsp coriander leaves chopped

TO SERVE
3 tbsp green mint, 2 tbsp red garlic & 5 tbsp tamarind chutney (see chutney section)

Methi na Muthiya fried : Recipe on page 31, Bhelpuri with chutneys ➤

1. Heat oil in a kadhai. Reduce flame and add red chilli powder and turmeric powder. Stir and add murmura and stir fry.
2. Add roasted ground nuts, salt and stir till murmura turns crisp.
3. Remove from fire and cool in a large mixing bowl.
4. Add sev, roasted channa dal, some crushed puris, chopped onion and potato. Add some coriander.
5. Add all the three chutnies, mix thoroughly and quickly. Check taste.
6. Garnish with sev, chopped onion and fresh coriander leaves. Serve immediately.

Note: Use puris from the recipe of sev-puri.

Methi na Muthia Fried

Makes 30 pieces   *Picture on page 29*

Muthiya, which means the snack is made using the fist (muthi) of the hand.

2 cups wheat flour, ¼ cup suji, ¼ cup besan
3 tbsp oil, ¼ cup curd
2 tsp chilli-ginger paste, 1 cup chopped methi leaves

DRY INGREDIENTS
1 tsp sugar, ½ tsp haldi (turmeric powder)
1 tsp chilli powder, 1 tsp dhania powder
¼ tsp hing (asafoetida), ¼ tsp soda-bi-carb, 2 tsp salt

1. Mix wheat flour, suji, besan with all dry ingredients.
2. Add oil, curd, chilli-ginger paste, methi leaves and mix well.
3. Add just enough water to the mixture to make a firm dough.
4. Take a small marble sized ball of the dough in the palm (mutthi) and press with fingers to make muthia. Heat oil for deep frying. Add 8-10 muthias at a time in hot oil. Reduce heat. Fry on low heat till brown.

Amiri Khaman

Serves 6

Crumbled Dhokla, tempered with mustard seeds and topped with fine sev.

1 cup channa dal - soak for 4-5 hours
1 tsp sugar, 1¼ tsp salt
1 tsp soda-bi-carb
juice of ½ lemon, or to taste

PASTE
7-8 flakes garlic, 4 green chillies, 1" piece ginger

TEMPERING
3 tbsp oil
1 tsp rai (mustard seeds), a pinch hing (asafoetida) powder
10 flakes garlic - finely chopped

GARNISH
thin sev, chopped coriander leaves and grated coconut

1. Wash and soak channa dal for 4-5 hours.
2. Keeping aside 2 tbsp dal, grind the rest of the dal to a coarse paste with about ¼ cup water.
3. To the ground dal add the ginger-chilli-garlic paste. Also add sugar, salt, soda-bi-carb and 2 tbsp soaked dal. Mix well. Keep aside covered to ferment for atleast 5 hours.
4. Add juice of lemon and mix.
5. Spread the mixture in a thali and steam for about 10-12 minutes till done.
6. Cool and crumble the dhokla. Add some powdered sugar, salt and lemon juice to taste.
7. To temper, heat oil. Add mustard seeds, hing and chopped garlic to oil. When garlic turns light brown, remove from fire and pour over the crumbled dhokla. Mix well.
8. Serve hot sprinkled with thin sev and garnished with chopped coriander leaves and grated coconut.

Pattise

Serves 4-6

Boiled potato balls stuffed with fresh coconut, cashewnuts and raisins.

4 medium sized potatoes - boiled
2 tbsp cornflour
3/4 tsp salt, or to taste

FILLING
1 tsp oil or ghee
1 tsp saunf (fennel seeds)
4 tbsp fresh grated coconut
7-8 cashewnuts - chopped, 12-15 raisins
½ tsp sugar
1 tbsp finely chopped green coriander
2 green chillies - deseeded and finely chopped
¼ tsp salt, or to taste

1. Mash potatoes and add cornflour and salt. Mix thoroughly and make 10 balls.
2. To prepare the filling, heat oil or ghee, add saunf followed by the remaining ingredients. Stir for 2-3 minutes.
3. Cool the filling and divide into 10 equal portions.
4. Flatten a potato ball, put a portion of the filling in the centre, gather the sides and shape it into a ball.
5. Heat the oil and deep fry 2-3 balls at a time on medium heat till light brown. Serve pattise with coconut chutney.

Pani Puri

Picture on cover   *Serves 4*

Delicious golgappas stuffed with sprouted moong & served with poodina pani.

DOUGH FOR THE PURIS
½ cup suji (fine), ½ cup maida (plain flour)

1. Mix maida and suji and knead a stiff dough with about ¼ cup water. Cover dough with wet muslin cloth and keep aside for 2 hours.
2. Take tiny marble sized balls of dough and roll each into thin puris of 1½" diameter.
3. Heat oil in a kadhai and fry puris immediately. (puri should not get dry). Keep the dough covered. Fry puris on low heat, turning twice till golden brown. Store puris in an air tight container.

FILLING
1 cup sprouted moong - boiled or steamed, 1 large potato - boiled & chopped
some imli (tamarind) chutney

POODINA PANI

50 gm pudina or mint leaves (2 bunches), 2 tbsp fresh coriander leaves
1 green chilli, juice of one lemon
2 tsp black salt, 1½ tsp salt
1 tsp jeera (cumin seeds)
7-8 saboot kali mirch (black peppercorns)
½ tsp saunf (fennel seeds)

1. Grind all the ingredients to a fine paste.
2. Add 2 cups of water to this paste and mix well. Chill pani.
3. To serve, make a hole in the centre of a puri, fill some boiled moong and potato. Add a spoonful of tamarind chutney and fill it with poodina pani.

Note: To make puris, you might get tempted to roll out a big round and then cut into smaller rounds with a sharp lid or a biscuit cutter. But this will not work. Although it is going to take longer, each puri has to be rolled individually.

Sev Puri

Serves 4 (25 puris)

A speciality of Bombay! Papadis in chutney sprinkled with fine sev namkeen.

DOUGH FOR PURIS
1 cup maida
1 cup wheat flour
2 tsp oil
½ cup water
oil for frying

TOPPING
2 boiled potatoes - mashed and mixed with a little salt
50 gm fine sev namkeen
green chutney, tamarind chutney (see chutney section)
1 chopped onion, 1 chopped tomato
1 tbsp chopped green coriander leaves

1. To prepare the puris, mix maida and wheat flour. Add oil and rub with the finger tips. Add just enough water to make a stiff dough.
2. Roll small thin puris of 2" diameter.
3. Prick them 2 to 3 times with a fork.
4. Heat oil in a kadhai. Fry puris on slow heat until light brown.
5. To serve, arrange the puris in a serving plate. Place 1 tsp of salted mashed potato on each puri.
6. Sprinkle sev on the puris.
7. Sprinkle green and tamarind chutney.
8. Garnish with chopped onion, tomato and coriander. Serve immediately.

Note: To make puris, you might get tempted to roll out a big round and then cut into smaller rounds or puris with a sharp lid or a biscuit cutter. But this will not work. Although it is going to take longer, each puri has to be rolled individually.

Ragda Pattise

Picture on back cover   *Serves 4*

Potato tikkis topped with a delicious lentil gravy.

PATTISE
6 medium size potatoes (½ kg) - boiled & mashed
3 tsp cornflour, 1 tsp salt, or to taste

RAGDA
1 cup dry peas - soaked overnight
1 tbsp oil, a pinch of hing (asafoetida), ½ tsp rai (mustard seeds)
1 onion - finely chopped, a few curry leaves
1" piece ginger and 3-4 garlic flakes (optional) - crushed to a paste or 1½ tsp
ginger-garlic paste
½ tsp haldi (turmeric powder), 1 tsp red chilli powder
1 tsp jeera powder
2 tsp dhania powder, 1 tsp garam masala
1½ tsp salt, or to taste

TO SERVE
green mint chutney, tamarind chutney (see section on chutneys)
some chopped coriander and finely chopped onion, optional

1. To prepare the pattise, mix potatoes with salt and cornflour. Make 8 big lemon sized balls. Flatten the balls slightly. Heat 4 tbsp oil in a frying pan or tawa and shallow fry them till brown and crisp.
2. To prepare the ragda, drain the water from the peas and pressure cook peas with 1½ cups water. After the first whistle, keep on slow fire for 10 minutes. Remove from fire.
3. Heat 2 tbsp of oil. Add rai. Let it splutter.
4. Add hing, chopped onion and stir fry for 2 minutes. Add curry leaves and ginger-garlic paste. Stir fry till onion turns light brown.
5. Add haldi, red chilli, jeera & dhania powder. Mix and add 1 cup water.
6. Add boiled peas and salt. Simmer for 5-7 minutes. Add garam masala, mix and remove from fire.
7. To serve, place 2 fried pattise in a plate. Pour 4 tbsp ragda over it. Pour a spoonful of green chutney and a spoonful of tamarind chutney. Garnish with chopped coriander leaves and finely chopped onion.

Muthia Bafela (Steamed)

Serves 6

Steamed rolls of bottle gourd and 3 kinds of flours

1 cup wheat flour, 1 tbsp suji or semolina, 2 tbsp besan (gram flour)
1 cup finely grated doodhi/lauki (white gourd)
1 tbsp finely chopped coriander leaves
3 tbsp oil
1 tsp sugar, 1 tsp lemon juice
¼ tsp haldi (turmeric powder), ½ tsp red chilli powder, 1 tsp dhania powder
1½ tsp salt, ¼ tsp soda-bi-carb

GRIND TO PASTE
2 green chillies, ½" piece ginger

TEMPERING
2 tsp oil, 1 tsp rai (mustard seeds)
1 tsp til (sesame seeds)

1. Mix wheat flour, suji, besan in a bowl.
2. Add grated lauki and ginger-chilli paste. Mix well.
3. Add all the other ingredients, except those for tempering.
4. Bind the mixture together. Add 1-2 tbsp water if required.
5. Apply some oil to the hands and make a thick, long roll of about 6-8" length from the mixture.
6. Steam the roll. To steam the rolls, boil water in a pan. Place a metal strainer on the pan of boiling water and place the roll in the strainer. Cover with a lid and steam the roll till done. To steam in a pressure cooker, after the first whistle keep it on slow fire for 7-8 minutes. A tooth pick inserted in the roll should come out clean when the roll is done.
7. Cool and cut the roll into ½" thick slices.
8. Heat a frying pan with oil. Add rai. As the rai splutters add til.
9. Add the muthia slices and saute for a while. Serve.

Kadhi and Dal

Gujurati Dals and Kadhis are thin and well blended. The sweet and sour Gujarati dal is wonderful! Small amounts of peanuts or peas add crunch to the smooth dal.

Gol Kadhi

Serves 2-3

A thin curry made from raw mangoes.

2 tbsp pulp of boiled raw mango
2 tbsp atta (wheat flour), 1 tbsp ghee
2 tbsp gur (jaggery)
½ tsp haldi (turmeric powder), ½ tsp chilli powder, 1 tsp salt
1 tbsp ghee, 1 tsp jeera (cumin seeds), 2-3 laung (cloves), 2" stick dalchini

1. Heat 1 tbsp ghee. Add wheat flour. Roast till pink. Remove from fire.
2. Add 2 cups water, stir and mix well so that no lumps are formed.
3. Add mango pulp, jaggery, turmeric, chilli powder and salt.
4. Return to fire and cook stirring continuously till it boils. Simmer for 5-7 minutes on low heat. Remove from fire.
5. For tempering, heat 1 tbsp ghee. Add jeera, laung and dalchini. As jeera turns golden add this tempering to the kadhi. Serve hot with rice.

Dapka Kadhi

Picture on facing page   *Serves 4*

Unfried moong balls in kadhi. Enjoy it without guilt with rice!

KADHI
2 tbsp besan (Bengal gram flour)
2 cups fresh curd
2 tsp chilli-ginger paste, ½ tsp sugar, 2 tsp salt, or to taste
2 tbsp chopped coriander

DAPKAS
½ cup dhuli moong dal (split green gram) - soaked for 4-5 hours
½ tbsp oil, ½ tsp green chilli-ginger paste
¼ tsp sugar, ¼ tsp eno fruit salt, ½ tsp salt, or to taste

TEMPERING
2 tbsp oil
3/4 tsp jeera (cumin seeds), 3/4 tsp rai (mustard seeds)
a pinch hing (asafoetida), 1 red chilli - broken into pieces

1. Soak the moong dal in lukewarm water for 4-5 hours or overnight. Drain well to remove all water. Grind the soaked moong dal to a very fine paste in a small spice blender.
2. Add the oil, green chilli-ginger paste, sugar, eno fruit salt and salt. Beat well for 2-3 minutes till light. Keep it aside.
3. Mix the besan, curds and 3 cups of water till smooth.
4. Add the green chilli-ginger paste, fresh coriander, sugar and salt and put to boil in a kadhai. Simmer for a while stirring occasionally.
5. When the kadhi is boiling, add in the dapka batter a little at a time using your fingers to form dumplings. Keep the kadhi boiling on low heat for 8-10 minutes till the dapkas float and also get cooked. Remove kadhi from fire and keep aside.
6. Heat oil for tempering. Reduce heat. Add jeera, rai and hing. When jeera turns golden, remove from fire and mix in the red chilli bits.
7. Add the tempering to the hot kadhi. Sprinkle fresh coriander. Serve.

Khati Mithi Dal

Serves 4

1 cup arhar (toovar) dal
2 tsp green chilli-ginger paste
½ tsp haldi (turmeric powder), 1 tsp dhania powder
6-7 curry leaves, 2 tbsp green peas, ½ tsp red chilli powder, 2 tsp salt
1 tbsp gur (jaggery), ¼ cup tamarind juice, or to taste
1 tbsp oil, ½ tsp rai (mustard seeds), 2 red chillies, a pinch of hing

1. Wash dal and pressure cook dal with 2 cups of water. After the first whistle, cook on low heat for 10 minutes. Remove from fire. When the pressure drops, mash thoroughly.
2. Add 3 cups water, chilli-ginger paste, turmeric, chilli powder, coriander powder, salt, green peas and curry leaves.
3. Bring dal to a boil and add jaggery and tamarind juice. Give 2-3 boils.
4. To temper, heat 1 tbsp oil, add ½ tsp mustard seeds and a pinch of hing and red chilli pieces. Let the mustard seeds crackle. Add to the hot dal. Garnish with grated coconut and chopped coriander leaves.

Gujarati Dal

Picture on page 1   *Serves 6-8*

Sweet and sour dal. The longer this dal is simmered, the better it tastes.

2 cups arhar (toovar dal)
2 tbsp peanuts

TEMPERING
2 tbsp ghee, 1 tbsp oil
¼ tsp hing (asafoetida)
½ tsp rai (mustard seeds), ½ tsp jeera (cumin seeds)
¼ tsp methi daana (fenugreek seeds)
a few curry leaves
2-3 laung, 2 stick dalchini (cinnamon)
2 small boriya (dry, round red chillies)

GARNISHING
some chopped coriander

OTHER INGREDIENTS
8 pieces cocum - soaked
1 tomato - chopped
2 tbsp gur (jaggery), adjust to taste
juice of 1 lemon
2" piece of ginger - chopped finely
4 green chillies - slit
½ tsp red chilli powder, ½ tsp haldi (turmeric powder)
3-4 tsp salt, or to taste

1. Wash and pressure cook the dal with peanuts in 4 cups of water. After the first whistle, keep on low flame for 5 minutes.
2. When the dal is cooked, cool slightly and blend till it is smooth.
3. Prepare the tempering by heating the ghee and oil in a big kadhai. Add hing, rai, jeera, methi daana, laung and dalchini. Let jeera turn brown. Add curry leaves & whole red chillies.
4. Reduce heat. Add cocum, tomato, jaggery, lemon juice, ginger, green chilli, chilli powder and haldi. Cook for 1-2 minutes.
5. Add 4 cups of water, dal, salt and simmer for 5-7 minutes. Serve hot garnished with coriander.

Gujarati Kadhi

Picture on page 1 **Serves 4**

2 cups curd, 2 cups water, 1½ tbsp besan (gram flour)
1 tsp green chilli-ginger paste, 1 tsp sugar, ¼ tsp haldi, 1 tsp salt

TEMPERING
1 tbsp ghee, 1 tsp jeera (cumin seeds)
1" dalchini (cinnamon), 4-6 laung (cloves)
7-8 curry leaves, 1 tbsp chopped coriander leaves

1. Beat curd till smooth. Add water, besan, chilli-ginger paste, turmeric powder, salt, sugar and mix well. Transfer to a heavy bottomed pan or a kadhai. Cook on medium heat stirring continuously. Add curry leaves, cook till it starts boiling. Simmer on low heat for 4-5 minutes. Remove from fire and keep aside.
2. Heat ghee. Add jeera. As jeera turns golden, add laung and dalchini. Add curry leaves. Pour ghee into the kadhi. Add coriander. Cover for a while. Serve hot with rice.

Panchkuti Dal

Serves 4

¼ cup toovar dal (pigeon peas), ¼ cup dhuli moong dal (split green gram)
¼ cup saboot moong (green gram), 2 tbsp urad dal, 2 tbsp channa dal
3 tbsp oil or ghee
½ tsp hing (asafoetida), 1 tsp jeera (cumin seeds), 3 laung, 1 tej patta
2 whole red chillies - broken into pieces
1 onion - finely chopped, 2 green chillies - finely chopped
6-8 flakes garlic - finely chopped, 1 tsp ginger - chopped
1 tomato - finely chopped, ½ tsp chilli powder, ¼ tsp haldi (turmeric) powder
juice of 1 lemon, salt to taste

1. Pressure cook dals in 4 cups of water for 5 minutes after the first whistle.
2. Heat oil, add hing, jeera, laung, tej patta & red chillies.
3. Add onions, green chillies, garlic and ginger and fry for few minutes.
4. Add tomatoes, chilli powder and haldi. Cook till oil separates. Add dals and water as desired. Add the lemon juice, salt and simmer for 10 minutes. Serve hot garnished with coriander.

VEGETABLES

Gujuratis generally being vegetarians, a lot of importance is given to fresh vegetables. 3 to 4 varieties of vegetables are cooked at a time for a meal. Onion and garlic are optional. In South Gujarat onion, garlic and fresh coconut are used liberally. In North Gujarat (Saurashtra) where green vegetables are less, more emphasis is given to pickles.

Rajwadi Bataka nu Shak

Serves 4   *Picture on page 2*

6 medium potatoes
1 tbsp khus khus (poppy seeds)
1 tbsp til (sesame seeds)
20 kishmish (raisins), 10 cashewnuts - split into 2 halves
1½ tsp lemon juice, 1 tsp sugar
1 tsp chilli powder, 1 tsp salt, 2 tbsp ghee

1. Peel potatoes, wash and cut into thin long fingers, about ¼" thick.
2. Heat 3 tbsp ghee in a kadhai and stir fry potato chips till golden brown and get cooked. Remove and place chips in bowl.
3. In the remaining ghee fry cashews, kishmish, til and khus khus on low heat for 1-2 minutes only.
4. Mix all the fried ingredients with fried chips.
5. Add chilli powder, sugar, salt, lemon juice and mix well.

Note: This vegetable is specially made for a wedding lunch or dinner.

Undhiya

Picture on facing page　　　　*Serves 5-6*

Favourite Gujarati mixed vegetable made from Surati beans (green beans), brinjals, potatoes, kand, sweet potatoes and bananas.

250 gm surti papadi (green broad beans or sem ki phalli)
100 gm (1 small) sweet potato - peeled and cut into 1" pieces
200 gm blue kand or jimikand - peeled and cut into 1" pieces
4-6 (100 gm) small brinjals, 3-4 small (100 gm) small potatoes, 1 banana
4-5 methina muthiya - recipe on page 31
6 tbsp oil

GRIND TOGETHER TO A MASALA
50 gm coriander leaves - chopped (1 cup)
2-3 tbsp grated coconut
2-3 green chillies, 1" piece ginger, 2-3 garlic flakes, 1 tsp ajwain
2 tbsp dhania powder, 1 tsp jeera (cumin seeds) powder
1 tsp red chilli powder, ½ tsp haldi (turmeric powder)
1 tsp sugar, 1½ tsp salt, 2 tsp lemon juice

SPRINKLE ON BEANS
a pinch of soda bi carb, ½ tsp ajwain (carom seeds), ¼ tsp salt

TEMPERING
6 tbsp oil, ¼ tsp hing (asafoetida), 1 tsp ajwain (carom seeds)

1. String the green broad beans (surati papdi), taking care not to separate the two sides. Wash the beans, sprinkle ½ tsp ajwain, a pinch of soda bi carb and ¼ tsp salt. Mix well.
2. Peel blue kand and sweet potatoes and cut into 1" pieces.
3. Peel potatoes, wash. Make 2 criss-cross slits on the whole potatoes and brinjals also.
4. Cut the banana into 1" pieces and make a slit in each piece.
5. Grind all ingredients of the masala together. Mix 4 tbsp oil.
6. Fill half of this masala into slits of brinjals, potatoes and bananas. Spread some masala on the green beans also. Mix some masala with the kand and sweet potatoes too. Keep the remaining masala for later use.

Contd....

7. Heat 6 tbsp oil in a big heavy bottomed pan, with a tight fitting lid.
8. Add 1 tsp ajwain and ¼ tsp hing.
9. Add half the beans forming the lower layer in the pan. Next put half of the brinjals and potatoes. Lastly put a layer of half the blue kand and sweet potatoes.
10. Add the rest of the beans, repeating the other 2 layers of potatoes and brinjals and last of all kand and sweet potatoes.
11. Add 3/4 cup water. Cover tightly and cook on low-medium heat for about 15 minutes.
12. Add banana pieces, muthias and the remaining masala. Add ½ cup of water. Stir carefully. Cover and cook on low heat for another 10 minutes till all the vegetables become tender and oil separates. Check salt.
13. Garnish with chopped coriander leaves and fresh grated coconut.

Vaingan Vatana nu Shak

Picture on page 77   *Serves 4*

Brinjal and green peas in a spicy masala.

1 medium (300 gms) tender brinjal of round big variety
1 cup shelled fresh green peas
½ tsp haldi (turmeric powder)
2 tsp dhania (coriander) powder
½ tsp chilli powder, ½ tsp jeera (cumin) powder
1 tsp salt or to taste
3 tbsp oil
pinch of hing (asafoetida)

PASTE
2 green chillies
1 tbsp fresh coriander leaves - chopped
4-5 flakes garlic
½" piece ginger

1. Wash and dice brinjal into 1" cubes.
2. Grind coriander, ginger, garlic and chilli into a paste.
3. Heat oil in kadhai and add hing.
4. Add cut brinjal, shelled peas and masala paste and saute for a minute.
5. Add all other ingredients and again saute for a minute.
6. Add ½ cup of water, cover and cook on low heat for 15-20 minutes.
7. Uncover and stir as brinjal and peas become tender and water dries up, remove from fire. Garnish with chopped coriander leaves. Serve.

Bhindi Stuffed

Picture on page 1   *Serves 4*

Lady fingers stuffed with a spicy coconut filling.

250 gm bhindi (lady fingers), small ones, 2-3" long

FILLING
½ cup besan
3-4 tbsp finely grated fresh coconut
1 tbsp very finely chopped or grated onion, optional
1 tbsp oil
1¼ tsp salt, 3/4 tsp red chilli powder
3 tsp dhania powder, ½ tsp haldi
½ tsp jeera (cumin seeds) powder

CHOWNK (TEMPERING)
2 tbsp oil
½ tsp jeera (cumin seeds), ¼ tsp hing (asafoetida)

1. Wash and wipe bhindi. Remove the ends and make a slit lengthwise.
2. Mix all ingredients of the filling together.
3. Stuff bhindis with this mixture.
4. To temper the bhindis, heat 2 tbsp oil in a big kadhai. Add ½ tsp jeera and ¼ tsp hing. Wait till jeera turns golden.
5. Put all the stuffed bhindis in hot oil, stir for 2-3 minutes.
   Cover and cook on low heat, for about 15-20 minutes, stirring occasionally, till bhindi becomes tender.
6. Garnish with fresh coriander and freshly grated coconut.

Vaingan Katri

Picture on page 67   *Serves 4*

Brinjal slices cooked with spicy green masala.

1 medium size brinjal, of big round tender variety
1 tsp besan (gram flour)
½ tsp haldi (turmeric powder)
2 tsp dhania powder
1 tsp jeera (cumin seeds) powder
½ tsp sugar, 1 tsp salt
a pinch of hing (asafoetida)
1 tsp oil

PASTE
8-10 flakes garlic
2 green chillies
3 tbsp coriander leaves chopped
2 tsp jeera (cumin seeds)

1. Cut brinjal vertically into two halves to get 2 round pieces, then cut each piece into half to get 4 round slices, approximately 1" thick.
2. Give superficial criss-cross cuts on both sides of all the brinjal slices.
3. Grind garlic, chillies, coriander leaves and jeera with just a tbsp of water to a fine paste.
4. To this ground paste, add besan, haldi, dhania powder, jeera powder, salt, sugar, hing and 1 tsp oil. Mix well.
5. Divide this masala into 8 equal portions.
6. Spread one portion of the masala on each side of a brinjal slice.
7. Heat a frying pan with 2-3 tbsp oil.
8. Put slices in the pan, cover and cook on medium heat for 5 minutes.
9. Uncover pan, turn the slices and add another 2 tbsp oil and cover. Cook for 5 minutes on medium heat.
10. Reduce heat, cook till brinjal slices become tender, turning carefully. Serve hot.

Tameta ni Katri

Picture on facing page   *Serves 4-6*

Good to look at and easy to make tomato cups.

4 big tomatoes
1 tsp oil, 1 tsp besan

GRIND TOGETHER TO A PASTE
8 flakes garlic
2 green chillies
2 tbsp coriander leaves chopped
1½ tsp jeera (cumin seeds)
2 tbsp dhania powder
½ tsp chilli powder, ¼ tsp haldi (turmeric powder)
½ tsp sugar, 1 tsp salt
a pinch of hing (asafoetida)

Vaingan Katri : Recipe on page 64, Tameta ni Katri ➢

1. Wash and cut tomatoes horizontally into two halves.
2. Grind all ingredients together to a fine paste.
3. Add 1 tsp each of besan and oil to the paste.
4. Make 8 equal portions of this masala.
5. Apply this masala, about 1 tsp full, on the cut surface of all tomato halves.
6. Spread 1 tsp oil in a nonstick frying pan. Keep on heat.
7. Put tomatoes with the cut side smeared with masala in the oil, cook uncovered for 3-4 minutes on low heat.
8. Then turn tomato slices very carefully (without disturbing masala layer). Then cover and cook for 4-5 minutes on low heat.
9. When the tomatoes get cooked, remove from fire.
   Garnish with chopped coriander leaves and serve hot with roti.

ONE MEAL DISH

Gujaratis prefer one meal dish for dinner.
Recipes given in this category are
substantial dishes. From nutritional point of
view these dishes are complete meals. They
contain cereals, lentils and vegetables.

Khichadi

Serves 6

2 cups rice
1 cup arhar or tur dal
1 onion - chopped (optional)
¼ cup groundnuts
2 tbsp ghee or oil
¼ hing powder (asafoetida)
3-4 laung (cloves)
2" stick dalchini (cinnamon)
1 tsp jeera (cumin seeds)
½ tsp haldi (turmeric powder)
2-3 whole, dry red chillies - broken into 2-3 pieces
3 tsp salt
7 cups water

1. Wash dal and rice and soak together for 30 minutes.
2. Heat 7 cups of water and keep aside.
3. Heat ghee in a pressure cooker, add hing, jeera, laung, dalchini and red chillies and saute for a few seconds.
4. Add chopped onion and saute till it becomes brown. Add groundnuts and turmeric powder.
5. Add soaked dal-rice mixture and salt. Saute for a minute.
6. Add hot water to rice-dal mixture, stir well.
7. Pressure cook to give 1 whistle. Reduce heat and keep on low heat for 10 minutes.
8. Serve hot with pure ghee and kadhi or vaghareli chhaas.

Dal Dhokli

Serves 4

Masala roti cooked in Tur dal.

DAL
1 cup tur (arhar) dal
2 tsp green chilli-ginger paste
½ tsp haldi (turmeric powder), 1 tsp dhania powder
6-7 curry leaves
2 tbsp green peas
½ tsp red chilli powder, 2 tsp salt
1 tbsp gur (jaggery), ¼ cup tamarind juice, or to taste

DOUGH FOR DHOKLI OR ROTI
2 cups wheat flour
1½ tsp chilli-ginger paste, 1 tbsp oil
½ tsp salt, ¼ tsp haldi (turmeric powder)
½ tsp ajwain (carom seeds), ½ tsp til (sesame seeds)

TEMPERING
1 tbsp oil, ½ tsp rai (mustard seeds)
2 to 3 whole, dry, red chillies, a pinch of hing (asafoetida)

GARNISH
1 tbsp fresh grated coconut and 1 tbsp chopped coriander leaves

1. Wash dal and pressure cook dal with 2 cups of water. After the first whistle, cook on low heat for 10 minutes.
2. Remove from fire. When the pressure drops, mash thoroughly.
3. Add 3 cups of water, chilli-ginger paste, turmeric, chilli powder, coriander powder, salt, green peas and curry leaves and keep it aside.

METHOD TO MAKE ROTIS (DHOKLIES)

1. Mix all ingredients of the dough together to a soft dough with enough water.
2. Make 6 rotis from this dough about 8" in diameter.
3. Cut the rotis into 1- 2" squares.
4. Bring dal to a boil and add jaggery and tamarind juice.

5. Add roti pieces one by one to the boiling dal. Stir occasionally, simmer for 15 minutes on low heat without covering. Remove from fire.
6. To temper, heat 1 tbsp oil, add ½ tsp mustard seeds and a pinch of hing and red chilli pieces. Let the mustard seeds crackle. Add to the hot dal.
7. Garnish with grated coconut and chopped coriander leaves. Serve hot with a dash of pure ghee.

Makai ni Khichdi

Serves 4

6 bhutte (tender whole corns) - peeled and grated
1 tsp sugar, salt to taste
juice of ½ lemon, 2 tbsp chopped coriander

TEMPERING
2 tbsp oil
1 tsp rai (mustard seeds), 1 tsp jeera (cumin seeds), ¼ tsp hing (asafoetida)
2 green chillies - chopped

1. Heat oil. Add rai, jeera, hing and green chillies and fry till seeds crackle.
2. Add the corn and cook on slow flame for 5 minutes.
3. Add enough water to cover the corn. Add sugar and salt. Cover and simmer till the corn is tender. Add more water if the khichdi looks thick.
4. Add lemon juice to taste and mix well. Garnish with coriander. Serve.

Handvo

Serves 6

A baked savoury cake made out of rice, lentils and vegetables.

2 cups rice
½ cup tur dal, ½ cup moong dal, ¼ cup chana dal
½ cup curd
1 cup grated white gourd (doodhi)
½ tsp haldi (turmeric powder), 1 tsp chilli powder, 3 tsp salt
2 tsp chilli-ginger paste
¼ tsp soda-bi-carb, ½ tsp lemon juice
2 tbsp oil

TEMPERING
1 tbsp oil
1 tsp rai (mustard seeds), 2 tsp til (sesame seeds)
2 red chillies - broken into bits, ¼ tsp hing (asafoetida)

Vaingan Vatana nu Shak : Recipe on page 60, Bhakri: Recipe on page 88 ➢

1. Wash and soak rice separately for 5-6 hours.
2. Wash and soak all dals together in another vessel for 5-6 hours.
3. Grind soaked rice coarsely with little water.
4. Grind soaked dals coarsely.
5. Mix rice & dal. Add curd & salt. Cover & ferment for 6-7 hrs or more.
6. In the fermented batter, add chilli-ginger paste, turmeric powder, chilli powder and grated doodhi and mix well. Heat ¼ cup with 2 tbsp oil and add to the fermented batter. Beat very well. Keep aside.
7. Grease a baking dish of 8" diameter (borosil) generously with oil. Heat oil in a small vessel, add rai. As rai starts spluttering add sesame seeds and pieces of red chillies and hing. Pour this oil into the baking dish and spread to cover the bottom. Keep dish aside.
8. Add soda-bi-carb to batter and add ½ tsp lemon juice over it.
9. Beat batter well and pour into the baking dish.
10. Bake at 220°C in a preheated oven for 35-40 minutes or till golden brown crust is formed. Remove from oven. Serve hot with curd.

Note: You can add some more vegetables like 1 cup green peas / 1 cup grated potato/½ cup ground nuts to the batter.

CHUTNEYS

Chutneys are used more as side dishes, but are nonetheless important because they provide nutritional value and variety of flavours and textures which are typical of Indian meals.

Chundo

Picture on page 1   *Serves 6-8*

Sweet chutney prepared from raw mangoes.

4 medium (500 gm) raw mangoes
1½ cups (250 gm) sugar
2 tsp red chilli powder
3/4 tsp haldi (turmeric powder)
1 tsp jeera (cumin seeds)
2 tsp salt

1. Peel and grate mangoes.
2. Add salt and haldi to grated mango and leave it for 3-4 hours.
3. Add sugar and cook on medium heat, stirring occasionally till it starts boiling.
4. Reduce heat, add chilli powder to the simmering mixture.
5. Cook till the chutney turns thick. Remove from fire.
6. Add jeera and stir. Fill in an airtight sterilized jar.

Red Garlic Chutney

Makes ½ cup

Served with bhel. Made from dry red chillies and garlic.

6 dry, red chillies
10 garlic flakes
1 tsp salt
1 tsp lemon juice

1. Soak dry red chillies in ½ cup water for 4-5 hours.
2. Drain chillies, reserving the water.
3. Grind the soaked chillies, garlic, salt and lemon juice with 2 tbsp of chilli water to a fine paste.
4. Remove from blender and add about 2-3 tbsp more of chilli water to make the chutney of a thin pouring consistency.

Green Mint Chutney

Serves 4

2 tbsp chopped green mango
4 green chillies
½ cup mint leaves chopped, ¼ cup chopped coriander leaves
2 tsp jeera (cumin seeds)
1 tsp sugar, 1 tsp salt

1. Peel and chop mango. Grind all ingredients together to a fine paste. Serve with snacks.

Note: If green mango is not available take 1 tbsp of lemon juice.

Green Coriander Chutney

Serves 4

Served with khaman dhokla or yellow dhokla. Made with coriander leaves, green chillies, ginger and sev.

100 gm fresh green coriander leaves (1½ cups chopped)
4 green chillies
1 tsp lemon juice
½" piece ginger
2 tbsp namkeen sev
½ tsp sugar
½ tsp salt

1. Grind all ingredients to a fine paste with 2 to 3 tbsp of water.

Date Tamarind Chutney

Makes 1 cup

Served with bhel and kachoris. Made from tamarind, dates and jaggery.

8-10 dates - wash, remove seeds and chop finely
½ cup imli (tamarind) - soaked in 1 cup hot water
½ cup gur (jaggery), or to taste
½ tsp jeera (cumin seeds) powder, ½ tsp chilli powder, 1 tsp salt, or to taste

1. Cook chopped dates in ½ cup water till they become tender. Mash them and pass through a metal sieve to get date pulp.
2. Mash tamarind. Pass the pulp through a sieve into the date pulp.
3. Add jaggery. Boil the mixture, add jeera, chilli powder and salt. Simmer on low heat till it reaches the right consistency.
4. Remove from fire. Cool and fill in a clean, dry jar. Store in a refrigerator.

ROTIS

There are a variety of rotis in Gujarati cuisine. Theplas are very thin whereas Bhakri is a small thickish roti. Gujaratis enjoy puris also.

Masala Puris

Serves 4-6

1½ cups atta (wheat flour)
¼ cup maida (plain flour), ¼ cup suji (semolina) fine
2 tbsp oil
1 tsp red chilli powder, ¼ tsp haldi (turmeric powder)
1 tsp jeera (cumin seeds), 1 tsp ajwain (carom seeds), 1 tsp salt

1. Mix atta, suji and maida. Add all other ingredients.
2. Add enough water and make a firm dough.
3. Take small portions of dough and roll out medium puris of 4" diameter.
4. Fry them in hot oil. Serve with Chundo.

Methi Masala Puri

Add ¼ cup chopped methi leaves and ½ tsp sugar to the dough.

Methi Thepla

Makes 8-9   *Picture on page 1*

1 cup wheat flour
¼ cup curd, 1 tbsp oil
½ cup chopped methi (fenugreek) leaves
¼ haldi (turmeric powder), ½ tsp chilli powder, 1 tsp salt, ½ tsp sugar

1. Mix all ingredients with wheat flour. Add about ¼ cup water to make a soft dough. Keep aside for 15-20 minutes.
2. Divide dough into 8-9 equal portions. Roll out each portion very thinly to get a 6" diameter roti. Cook on a hot tawa using a little oil or ghee. Serve either hot or cold with chundo (aam ki chutney) or in the thali.

Masala Thepla

Add ajwain (carom seeds) and til (sesame seeds), omit methi and sugar.

Bhakri

Picture on page 77   *Makes 8-10*

Thick, small rotis which taste like tandoori roti

2 cups wheat flour
2 tbsp oil
½ cup water, or as required

1. Rub oil into wheat flour.
2. Sprinkle water and make a firm dough.
3. Make 10 small lemon sized balls.
4. Roll out each ball into thick rotis of 4" diameter.
5. Cook on a hot griddle (tawa) and then on direct flame like a phulka.
6. Apply ghee and serve hot.
7. Serve with any vegetable or dal.

DRINKS

Gujaratis start their meals with butter milk (chhaas). Sometimes it is tempered with cumin and chopped fresh coriander.

Chhaas

Serves 4

A delicious spiced buttermilk.

2 cups fresh curd
½ tsp black salt, 1 tsp sugar
salt to taste
1 tsp bhuna jeera (roasted cumin) powder
½ tsp green chilli-ginger paste
1 tbsp coriander leaves - very finely chopped

1. Beat curd till smooth.
2. Add all other ingredients and mix well.
3. Add 4 cups cold water and whisk well. Serve.

Vaghareli Chhaas

Serves 4   *Picture on page 1*

Chhaas or buttermilk tempered with asafoetida and cumin.

CHHAAS
2 cups fresh curd
½ tsp black salt, 1 tsp sugar, 1 tsp salt, or to taste
1 tsp bhuna jeera (roasted cumin) powder, ½ tsp green chilli-ginger paste
2 tbsp finely chopped coriander

TEMPERING
2 tsp oil
a pinch of hing, 3/4 tsp jeera (cumin seeds), 10-15 curry leaves - chopped

1. Beat curd till smooth. Add all other ingredients given under chhaas and mix well. Add 4 cups cold water and whisk well.
2. To temper, heat oil. Add hing. Add jeera. Remove from fire. Add curry leaves. Pour oil into the chhaas. Serve.

Panha

Serves 4-6

½ kg (4 medium) raw mangoes
3/4 cup sugar, or to taste
½ tsp chhoti illaichi (green cardamom) powder
a pinch of kesar (saffron)

1. Boil the raw mangoes in water till they are very soft.
2. Drain all the water. Remove the skin from the mangoes.
3. Remove pulp from mangoes. Strain the mango pulp.
4. Add the sugar, cardamom powder and saffron and mix well.
5. Store in a bottle and refrigerate.
6. When you wish to serve, put 2-3 tbsp of the mixture into a glass and top up with chilled water.

Note: Instead of the cardamom and saffron, you can add cumin powder and black salt.

Sweets

Gujaratis are very fond of sweets. Mohan thal, a mithai, is very popular.

Mohan Thal

Picture on facing page   *Serves 4*

A mithai made from besan, ghee, khoya and sugar.

1 cup besan (gram flour), 2 tbsp milk
1 cup khoya (mawa)
½ cup ghee
1 tsp cardamom powder

SUGAR SYRUP
1 cup sugar
½ cup water

TOPPING
a silver sheet
4-5 sliced almonds, 8-10 pistachios

Basundi : Recipe on page 97, Mohan Thal ➤

1. Sprinkle milk on besan and mix thoroughly with fingers. Leave it for 10-15 minutes.
2. Pass this besan through a metal sieve with big holes, so that the besan becomes granular.
3. Heat ½ cup ghee in a heavy bottomed pan, add besan and roast on slow heat for 10-15 minutes till it becomes golden and leaves aroma.
4. Add khoya to this mixture and mix well. Saute for few minutes. Remove from fire.
5. Mix sugar and water in a pan and simmer for 7-8 minutes till the syrup reaches one thread consistency. To see that it has become one thread consistency, lift some syrup with a spoon and let it trickle down. If the syrup is dense and leaves a thread like consistency, it is ready to be used. Remove from fire.
6. Add besan-khoya mixture to sugar syrup.
7. Mix cardamom powder and mix well.
8. Spread the hot mixture into a greased 6" diameter thali. Press a silver sheet on top. Sprinkle almonds and pistachios on top. Cool and cut into 1½" squares.

Basundi

Serves 4-5   *Picture on page 95*

Rabdi or thickened sweetened milk, flavoured with cardamoms and saffron.

1 kg milk (full cream or whole milk)
a few strands of kesar (saffron), optional
¼ cup sugar, or slightly less than ¼ cup
½ tsp chhoti illaich (green cardamom) powder
4-6 cashewnuts - cut into small pieces
4-6 almonds and pista - sliced, 1 tsp chironji

1. Boil milk with kesar in a thick bottomed or a nonstick vessel, stirring occasionally on medium heat. Cook for about 30 minutes till the milk reduces to half.
2. Add sugar and continue simmering on low heat for 12-15 minutes till the milk becomes thick.
3. Remove from fire. Add cardamom powder, cashewnut pieces, sliced almonds and chironji. Serve hot or cold.

Doodhino Halwo

Serves 4

Grated lauki, cooked in ghee with khoya.

1 very small (250 gm) doodhi (white gourd, lauki)
1 tbsp ghee
2-3 laung (cloves)
2" stick dalchini (cinnamon)
¼ cup sugar, or slightly more
200 gm khoya - crumbled
2 tbsp kishmish - soaked in water
4-5 almond - sliced, to garnish
seeds of 4 chhoti illaichi (cardamoms) - powdered

1. Peel and grate the white gourd.
2. Heat ghee in a heavy bottomed kadhai.
3. Add laung and dalchini. Wait for a minute.
4. Add grated doodhi. Mix. Cover and cook the doodhi on slow fire for about 15 minutes, stirring occasionally.
5. Add sugar and stir for 5 minutes on medium heat till water dries.
6. When water dries up add kishmish and khoya. Bhuno for 5-7 minutes.
7. Remove from fire and add cardamom powder and mix well. Garnish with almonds. Serve.

Kesari Shrikhand

Picture on page 1   *Serves 6*

1 kg curd (thick and fresh) of full cream milk
1 cup (150 gm) sugar - powdered
¼ tsp kesar (saffron) - soaked in 1 tbsp warm milk for 5 minutes
½ tsp cardamom powder
¼ tsp nutmeg powder
2 tbsp cream
4-5 almonds and 4-5 pistachios - sliced

1. Tie the freshly set curd in a muslin cloth for 3-4 hours.
2. Pass this curd through a sieve (soup strainer) to make it smooth.
3. Add powdered sugar, cardamom, nutmeg, saffron, cream and mix well.
4. Garnish with kesar, sliced almonds and pistachios. Serve cold.

Amrakhand

Serves 6

Shrikhand flavoured with fresh mango pulp.

1 kg curd (thick and fresh) of full cream milk
1 cup thick mango pulp
1¼ cups (200 gm) sugar - powdered, or to taste
few drops mango essence

1. Tie the freshly set curd in a muslin cloth for 3-4 hours.
2. Pass this curd through a sieve to make it smooth.
3. Add sugar, mango pulp, essence and mix well. Serve cold.

Note: Alfanso mango gives best result.

Fruit Shrikhand

Serves 6

Shrikhand with banana, apples, grapes, chickoos.

1 kg curd (thick and fresh) of full cream milk
1 cup (150 gm) sugar - powdered
2 tbsp cream
½ tsp cardamom powder
1 sliced banana, 2 chickoos - diced
½ cup seedless grapes
2 tbsp diced pineapple
1 apple - diced, 2 tbsp ripe mango - diced

1. Tie the freshly set curd in a muslin cloth for 3-4 hours.
2. Pass this curd through a metal sieve (soup strainer) to make it smooth.
3. Add sugar and cardamom and mix well. Add cream.
4. Add all the fruits to shrikhand and mix. Serve chilled.

Wedhami

Makes 12-15

Puran poli. Small rotis stuffed with sweetened moong dal.

2 cups wheat flour, 2 tbsp oil
1 cup moong dal, 2 tbsp ghee, 1 cup sugar, 1 tsp cardamom powder

1. Add oil to flour and mix well. Add enough water to make a soft dough.
2. Clean and wash dal, cook in pressure cooker with 1½ cups water to give 1 whistle. Heat 2 tbsp ghee and add cooked dal & sugar. Cook on slow fire till dal becomes dry. Remove from fire. Cool. Add cardamom.
3. Roll out a ball from the dough into a 3" diameter circle. Place a portion of the filling mixture and fold the edges of the dough over the filling.
4. Flatten the dough and roll again into a 4" diameter circle.
5. Cook on a tawa over a medium flame till golden brown in colour on both sides. Smear with ghee and serve hot. Repeat with the remaining dough and filling.

BEST SELLERS BY

101 Paneer Recipes

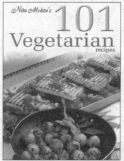

101 Vegetarian Recipes

SPECIAL Vegetarian Recipes

Cakes & Cake Decorations

101 International Recipes

Burgers & Sandwiches

Vegetarian MUGHLAI

Mother & Child Cookbook